A vital and necessary resource for all who want to understand where God fits into their world of work!

Brian Allenby
Christians at Work

Being a disciple is essential for any Christian at work - this book succinctly tells you why and brilliantly shows you how.

Sir Peter Vardy
The Vardy Foundation

Copyright © 2007 Graham Beynon

Published by 10Publishing, a division of 10ofthose.com.
13 Airport Road, Belfast BT3 9DY.

10 PUBLISHING
A DIVISION OF 10 OF THOSE.COM

www.10ofthose.com

The right of Graham Beynon to be identified as the author of this work has been asserted by her in accordance with the Copyright, Designs and Patents Act 1988.

Scripture taken from the HOLY BIBLE, TODAY'S NEW INTERNATIONAL VERSION®. Copyright © 2001, 2005 by International Bible Society®. Used by permission of International Bible Society®. All rights reserved worldwide. "TNIV" and "Today's New International Version" are trademarks registered in the United States Patent and Trademark Office by International Bible Society®. Use of either trademark requires the permission of International Bible Society.

All rights reserved. Except as may be permitted by the Copyright Act, no portion of this publication may be reproduced in any for or by any means without prior permission from the publisher.

ISBN 13: 978-1-906173-02-9

Design by: Jonathan Caplin **www.electrolyte.co.uk**
Print Management by: Print by Design Ltd **www.printbydesign.co.uk**

Jesus@Work:
Being a Disciple for Christ in the workplace

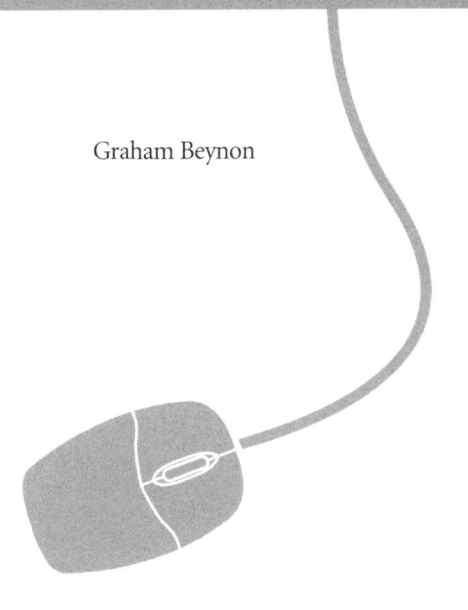

Graham Beynon

Contents

Introduction	8
1. The original job description	10
2. The small print	15
3. Thinking about Monday morning	20
4. Working on Tuesday afternoon	27
Further reading	37

Series Introduction

Jesus was supremely concerned that his followers might be both disciples and disciple makers. But in reality what does this mean? What does a true disciple look like? What does a true disciple do? What is the role of a disciple maker?

This series is designed to help Christians with those questions. Living as a disciple of Jesus Christ is not easy; there are many challenges and struggles, however, we do believe that God has equipped us with everything we need to live a life which is pleasing and honouring to Him.

In 2 Timothy Paul was able to write: '…the time has come for my departure. I have fought the good fight, I have finished the race, I have kept the faith. Now there is in store for me the crown of righteousness…'

We desire that this series might help us to be able to say the same thing when our departure from this life looms. These books seek to address some of the main issues that face a Christian disciple. The principles taught in this series are not based on good notions, but rather straightforward, biblical theology.

May it cause each of us to fight the good fight; finish the race; and keep the faith.

> *When it's all been said and done*
> *There is just one thing that matters*
> *Did I do my best to live for truth*
> *Did I live my life for You*
> *When it's all been said and done*
> *All my treasures will mean nothing*
> *Only what I've done for love's Reward*
> *Will stand the test of time*

Lord Your mercy is so great
That You look beyond our Weakness
And find purest gold in miry clay
Making sinners into saints

I will always sing Your praise
Here on earth and ever after
For You've shown me Heaven's my
True home
When it's all been said and done
You're my life when life is gone

Lord I'll live my life for You

Words and Music by Jim Cowan
© 1999 Integrity's Hosanna! Music

Jonathan Carswell

Introduction

You spend the majority of your life doing two things: one is sleeping, which if you're anything like me you enjoy a great deal and spend as much time as possible doing. The other of course is working, which many of us don't enjoy nearly as much, and often wish away, longing to be elsewhere.

But whether we enjoy our work or not, we can't avoid it. Work can be spoken of as any activity done to accomplish something that is needed, rather than activity which is done because it is enjoyable in itself. In other words, work is a means to an end. That doesn't mean you can't or won't ever enjoy your work; it simply means you have to do it.

On that basis we all spend a huge quantity of our life working. It might be in a paid job, or we might be studying at school or university, engaged in voluntary work or involved in the necessary and important task of bringing up a family with all that that entails. Even when retirement comes, we never really retire, as we may take on certain projects and responsibilities, and that constitutes work. And if we are unemployed we still 'work' - part of that may be looking for a job. When you think about it, the bulk of our days involve work.

But what does the Bible say about work? Many people don't make any connection between being a Christian and their day in the office or at home. But as it has often been pointed out, if we don't take our Christianity with us to work, we relegate it to a leisure activity. In effect we are saying that our Christian faith is not an integral part of our life.

The aim of this short book is to consider how we can be a Christian disciple at work. First we will look at what God says about work itself; this will then guide us in how we should think about it and apply it to our particular situation.

The material in this book stemmed from two sermons at my church on work. At the time I felt that such a topic was rarely addressed directly from the pulpit - I certainly hadn't heard any sermons on the topic myself. That was many years ago, and since then I've been able to discuss further, read more, and speak on the whole issue again. I am indebted to those who have stimulated and contributed to my own understanding, helping me to think through again the challenges and application of this important area of Christian discipleship.

My hope and prayer is that this book will help you think biblically about work, enabling you to live differently in whatever work you are engaged in.

1
The original job description

Why do we work?

> Imagine standing in the local high street armed with a questionnaire. The question you are asking everyone is, 'Why do you work?' What kind of answers might you get?

Whenever I've asked people that question the replies have fallen into two groups. One group says, 'I work because I have to.' It's true. You need to earn money to live; after all, you've got to pay the bills! Or it could be that you need to work because you can't escape your responsibilities: the children need looking after, the housework doesn't get done by itself and the coursework won't go away. But whatever the answer is, you need to work. And so in this first category, work is seen as a necessary evil. It's not something you particularly enjoy; in fact you would prefer not to be doing it at all, but you work because you have to.

Perhaps you can identify with that yourself. You groan on Monday mornings. This could be because your work is boring; you spend the day looking at the clock waiting for 5:30 to arrive. Or it might be because your work is too demanding and pressurised; you spend all day hoping you won't be home too late to help put the children to bed. But for whatever reason it is unpleasant, and we only do it because we have to.

However, a second group of replies run along different lines. They say, 'I work because I want to. I'd choose to be there on a Monday morning; I enjoy what I do and have real job satisfaction.' Some people realize that without work they'd just get bored. Others find that work is what gives them a purpose and meaning in life.

Maybe you can identify with this second group as well. You enjoy the work you do and the responsibilities you have. While there are moments you would like to escape, you don't groan each morning at the prospect ahead - you want to do it. Most people reading this will probably identify with aspects from both responses. You take some enjoyment in what you do with your days; there can be satisfaction, but there are great frustrations as well.

Is this to be expected? Is there a biblical view of work that makes sense of this mixed experience? Is there a view that gives us a more foundational reason as to why we should work in the first place? Yes there is. We were made to rule the world.

Made to rule the world

In the account of God's creation of the world we read:

> *Then God said, 'Let us make human beings in our image, in our likeness, so that they may rule over the fish in the sea and the birds in the sky, over the livestock and all the wild animals, and over all the creatures that move along the ground.'*
>
> *So God created human beings in his own image,*
> *in the image of God he created them;*
> *male and female he created them.*
>
> *God blessed them and said to them, 'Be fruitful and increase in number; fill the earth and subdue it. Rule over the fish in the sea and the birds in the sky and over every living creature that moves on the ground.'*
> Gen. 1:26-28

God said he would make people in his image. Look at the passage again. The first verse says that people are made in God's image so that they may rule over creation.

In effect God is saying, 'We'll make them in our image so they can be rulers like us.'

The world was made perfect; Adam and Eve were created in God's image and placed in the Garden of Eden to live. But still there is the idea that the world is incomplete. It needs to be subdued and controlled. In the passage above God says that we should increase in number, subdue the earth and rule over the creatures of the earth (verse 28). This command to govern, manage and take care of the world can also be found elsewhere in the Bible.

People put in charge

We see this idea again later on in the Old Testament. It is particularly clear in Psalm 8, which acts as a commentary on these verses in Genesis.

> *When I consider your heavens,*
> *the work of your fingers,*
> *the moon and the stars,*
> *which you have set in place,*
> *what are mere mortals that you are mindful of them,*
> *human beings that you care for them?*
>
> *You have made them a little lower than the heavenly beings*
> *and crowned them with glory and honour.*
> *You made them rulers over the works of your hands;*
> *you put everything under their feet:*
> *all flocks and herds,*
> *and the animals of the wild,*
> *the birds in the sky,*
> *and the fish in the sea,*
> *all that swim the paths of the seas.*
>
> **LORD**, *our Lord,*
> *how majestic is your name in all the earth!*
> Ps. 8:3-9

The psalmist looks at the creation and cannot believe the position God has given to us, as he responds with praise and adoration which is captured in this song of worship. 'You've made us rulers over the work of your hands. You've put everything under our feet!' And then he echoes Genesis 1 in listing the animals that we rule over.

So human beings are made to rule the world that God created. But how should we rule?

Ruling well

Imagine someone asked you to take care of their garden, or their house, or their pet while they go on holiday. In doing so they are putting you in charge.

But that doesn't give you an excuse to do what you want. You shouldn't then wreck the garden, trash the house, or kick the dog. You should rather look after those things as that person would want you to, because ultimately they are theirs not yours. You are in charge on their behalf.

We are to rule the earth as God would want us to. To rule as he himself would rule. This should give us reason to exercise this responsibility with great care. We are to work the land so that it produces crops for us; we are also to take care of the land so that we don't destroy it.

Workers because we are rulers

This is where the term 'work' comes in. In ruling the world as God's image bearers we need to see that this involves work. God appears in the opening chapters of Genesis as a God who works, who creates and forms the world in six days, and then rests from all his work.

Being made in his image, we are made to work too; we are designed to be creative, to be productive. The two go hand in hand. We are workers because we are rulers. This becomes clear in the second chapter of Genesis. Having created Adam, we read that 'The **LORD** God took the man and put him in the Garden of Eden to work it and take care of it' (Gen. 2:15).

Adam is to work the garden so that it is productive, and he is to keep it - that is watch over it, be in charge of it. This garden has great potential, but it won't achieve it by itself. It needs someone in charge. And that is the position God has given to Adam and also to us.

So how does this apply to us? The command is much broader than just working the land - all of our work, whatever this may involve, falls under this umbrella. Whether you manage the world's finances, develop the world's communication systems; whether you care for the world's sick, teach at a primary school or mend the world's roads, it's all part of working so as to rule the earth.

As the biblical narrative goes on, we see some people making tools, others building cities, some raising livestock, others making musical instruments. Technology, management, construction, art: they're all part of what God has made us for, part of why he's placed us on earth.

We work because it's intrinsic to our human nature, it is how God has made us, part of his original design. So there is nothing intrinsically bad about work - quite the opposite; it is made as a good part of God's creation.

Perfect rule and perfect work

In the beginning, before the devastating effects of sin, work would have been satisfying. I have no doubt that Adam and Eve would have looked forward to it each morning, taking immense pleasure in it. Similarly, the rule over creation would have been complete. Adam and Eve cared for the world and brought it to its full potential.

> Think about the most satisfying moment of any work you've done - the greatest fulfilment you ever had, and the sense of achievement you felt. That experience of control, of managing something and making it work well, was the only experience of work that Adam and Eve had at this point. That is how God made work.

Already we can see a fundamental difference in the Christian view of work to many ideas around us today. We shouldn't think of work as a bad thing to escape from, but rather a good part of creation. We shouldn't think of work as something we need to do simply for what we will gain (money or whatever other benefits there may be), but something we do because it is part of how we are made. God is the ultimate source of my particular job description, whatever it is, because he is the one who wrote the original job description as seen in Genesis 1.

However this idea of perfect rule and perfect work is not what we experience now. So what has gone wrong?

2

The small print

When God made the world it was all made perfect. God looked at it all and said that is was 'very good'. There was nothing wrong with it anywhere, and that included our work.

But Genesis 3 brings the great turning point. Adam and Eve, rather than trusting and believing God, are led to disbelieve and disobey him. Turning away from God and rebelling against his rule is what has wrecked God's perfect creation.

The effects are everywhere. Most foundationally, this rebellion affects our relationship with God. We are no longer in a relationship with him as our Father and King, where we live under his blessing. This is pictured most clearly in Genesis 3 by Adam and Eve being put out of the garden, and so out of relationship with God.

It also affects our relationship with each other. We were made to live in loving community with each other, but that has also been wrecked. Now there are arguments, tensions, factions, and envy amongst us. God didn't make us to hurt each other or fight each other - that is all part of the results of sin.

But it also affects our work. In the aftermath of our rebellion we read this:

> To Adam he said, 'Because you listened to your wife and ate from the tree about which I commanded you, "You must not eat of it,"
> > 'Cursed is the ground because of you;
> > through painful toil you will eat of it
> > all the days of your life.
> > It will produce thorns and thistles for you,
> > and you will eat the plants of the field.
> > By the sweat of your brow
> > you will eat your food

> *until you return to the ground,*
> *since from it you were taken;*
> *for dust you are*
> *and to dust you will return.'*
>
> Gen. 3:17-19

As a result of our sin the ground is cursed by God. And that means that working the ground will no longer be the delight God intended. Instead of easy work it will be 'painful toil'. The ground will no longer be readily compliant with Adam's attempts to work it; rather it will produce 'thorns and thistles' for him to contend with. It will be by the sweat of his brow that Adam will now grow his food. Peace and harmony with our work will be replaced with frustrations and hardship. And it is all because of our rebellion against God.

Frustrating work, incomplete rule

Rather than being the fulfilling experience it was supposed to be, work will be frustrating. That doesn't mean that there won't ever be elements of satisfaction to our work, only it won't be perfectly fulfilling as it was designed to be. To refer back to Genesis 3:18 again, our work often involves 'thorns and thistles'.

That terminology is used of course because Adam was a gardener, but if you think about your work I'm sure you can list some equivalents: the sheer tedium, the frustration of things not working out as they were supposed to, the wrestling with problems and physical exhaustion. Or the 'thorns and thistles' may be the exhaustion of working with difficult colleagues, or the weariness of trying to control unruly children; it may mean computers crashing, the boredom of the factory floor, or the pressure of management.

And similarly, our rule over the world will now be incomplete. We will never subdue the earth as we were supposed to. We will never take care of the world as God intended. Instead we will wreck the world in so many ways because of our selfish and evil intentions. More than that, the world itself has changed so that we will never bring it under control - it will continue to produce thorns and thistles for us no matter how much we try. It is hard for us to grasp this, and equally hard for us to imagine and understand what our perfect rule over the physical world would have looked like. Whatever it would have been like, it would certainly have been different from the state of the world today.

Do you see that what we are left with is a distortion of what God intended his world to be? Some of the original design is still there and we can still marvel with the psalmist at the marvels of creation, but the world is only a shadow of what it used to be. And that fits with our experience. We do still rule, but not completely. We exercise massive influence over the world, but it is not actually under our control.

The right view of work today

All of this is because of how God made work and how our rebellion has distorted it. Once we have grasped this, we should have a positive but also a very realistic view of work. We know how good it was made to be, how it is part of God's design, and so we don't shun or despise it. Rather we look to enjoy it where we can, and expect to find some satisfaction and delight in it.

But at the same time we know that it will never deliver the full satisfaction it was supposed to. There will always be thorns and thistles, whatever our work may involve. We are not surprised by set backs, frustration or exasperation with work.

Holding these ideas together is fundamental to our view of our work today. We don't let the good parts of work mean we worship it, but neither do we let the bad parts of work mean we despise it. We'll think about how it affects our approach and attitude in chapter 3, but first we need to finish the biblical picture on work.

Work restored

Thankfully, it is not always going to be like this. The Bible gives us a picture of the future, and it's a picture where all of sin's effects are undone, it's a picture where everything is made new. Both Isaiah and then John talk about a new heaven and a new earth, where everything is re-made. Jesus refers to this when he speaks about 'the renewal of all things' (Mt. 19:28). The word he uses there means renewing or rebirth, and pictures the transformation of all of creation.

When we think about the future for the Christian we usually speak about heaven. However, what we should really talk about is the 'new creation'. Heaven often seems vague and distant - floating around in a disembodied spiritual bliss. But speaking of a new creation reminds us that God is going to renew the physical world, which includes his giving us new physical bodies to live on this new earth.

As the effects of sin are overturned and God's curse on the ground ends, we will return to the position of God's image bearers who rule the earth under him. God's original design will be restored.

We are not told very much about what we will do in the new creation. In fact we are told little about life there. But there are some hints that we will work. Isaiah 65 talks of the new creation. This is part of what it says:

> *They will build houses and dwell in them;*
> > *they will plant vineyards and eat their fruit.*
> *No longer will they build houses and others live in them,*
> > *or plant and others eat.*
> > *For as the days of a tree,*
> > *so will be the days of my people;*
> > *my chosen ones will long enjoy*
> > *the work of their hands.*
> *They will not labour in vain,*
> > *nor will they bear children doomed to misfortune;*
> > *for they will be a people blessed by the* **LORD,**
> > *they and their descendants with them.*
>
> Is. 65:21-23

The main point being made here is that we will enjoy what our work has produced - we will plant vineyards and eat their fruit, and build houses and live in them, rather than having someone else take them over. Our days will be like a tree - which is an image of stability and longevity. We won't be uprooted but rather will continue to enjoy the work of our hands. And so it suggests that we will continue to work, but to work in a different way to now. We will not labour in vain.

All this points to a reversal of the curse of Genesis 3 so that our work returns to being the pleasurable, satisfying experience God made it to be. We don't know what form it might take, but work will be restored one day, and we will enjoy it as God meant us to.

Work in perspective

Now that we have the main biblical framework in place, we can think about how this should shape our thinking and approach to work. But before we end this chapter, here is a summary of the fundamental truths we have covered:

- God made you to work, it is a good part of his original design
- Work is now distorted by the effects of sin and will involve 'hard toil and labour'
- The whole creation, including our rule and work, will one day be renewed.

These won't be common assumptions round the office, on the factory floor or at the school gate. And so we will need to remind ourselves of them and consciously reflect on them.

> So what should our response be? As you start another working week, thank God for creating work. Praise him for making us in his image and giving us such a privileged position of rule in his creation. If you are feeling frustration or weary, remind yourself this is all part of what has gone wrong with the world - sin. And as you feel like your work is out of control, remind yourself of the new creation that is yet to come and the promise and hope that this brings; God's original design will one day be restored.

3
Thinking about Monday morning

Get on with your work

The biblical framework has now been set. So how should we approach our work as Christians? What sort of attitude should we have as Monday morning comes around again? The book of Proverbs tells us about a wise attitude to work. The recurring theme here is to simply get on with it. Let's consider some of the things it says:

> *Lazy hands make for poverty, but diligent hands bring wealth. (10:4)*
>
> *All hard work brings a profit, but mere talk leads only to poverty. (14:23)*
>
> *One who is slack in his work is a close relative of one who destroys. (18:9)*
>
> *The craving of sluggards will be the death of them, because their hands refuse to work. (21:25)*
>
> *Be sure you know the condition of your flocks, give careful attention to your herds; for riches do not endure for ever, and a crown is not secure for all generations. (27:23-24)*
>
> *Those who work their land will have abundant food, but those who chase fantasies will have their fill of poverty. (28:19)*

Again and again in these verses we see the expectation that people will work and will work hard. Regular work is how God expects us to provide for ourselves and our families.

These commands are practical and down to earth - people are for example advised to know the condition of their flocks (27:23-24). In other words, we should be careful with whatever our work involves, being diligent in it and attentive, keeping an eye on how it is going. There is also the expectation that hard work will bring the appropriate reward, whether in food and money.

We need to be careful here because the book of Proverbs doesn't always give promises; sometimes it is more an observation on life. So when we read that 'All hard work brings a profit' (14:23), we mustn't think that means we will all be rich as long as we put the hours in. But there is still the expectation that hard work is rewarded and the person who is prepared to work will be able to provide for themselves and their family.

You will have noticed that along with these encouragements to work there are warnings. The first four verses quoted caution us against laziness. Whilst our sinfulness affects our work in many ways, the prime one is laziness - many of us slack off in work when we should be working hard.

> I heard recently that the average time spent in productive work by someone in an office environment was less than an hour each day. Lots of time was spent chatting, making coffee, rearranging their desk, checking email, surfing the web or taking breaks. The Christian should consciously try to stand apart from that sort of culture and commit themselves to working hard.

Appreciate your work

We must appreciate work as a good part of creation. That is very different from the view expressed at the beginning of this book: 'I work because I have to.' Rather, the Christian says, 'I work because God made me to.' Much of the world around us thinks that life would be so good without work; the ideal life is 'work-free'. People talk about winning the lottery and so not having to work, or they say they can't wait until retirement. If you ask someone to describe paradise, they don't mention work. But the Christian knows that God's original paradise had work in it, and so will his final paradise.

So while many people around us will see work as a bad thing to escape from, the Christian should think of it as a good thing we should embrace.

Whereas the world lives for the weekend and says 'Thank God it's Friday', the Christian can live for the week and say 'Thank God it's Monday!'

Of course not everyone around us is negative about work, and you may feel that you are reasonably positive about work yourself. That is fine. But even then we need to think through why we are positive towards work. It is very easy to think of work as worthwhile because of the benefits it brings. You work so that you can gain more money or status or personal fulfilment or holidays - or whatever. You view work as worthwhile because of what you gain.

Christians can sometimes slide into a variation of this. I've heard people say that they have a good job because of its benefits. Yes, it allows them more time to be involved in church, or it provides great opportunities to witness; it also earns them lots of money which they can give away. Now don't get me wrong here; those are really great things to appreciate about a job, and they are reasons that might affect your choice of job. But the point is this: don't value your job only for its benefits, even if they are great Christian benefits. It is a good gift from God. It is worthwhile in itself, no matter what gains there are or aren't.

Don't worship your work

Perhaps you smiled as you read the heading above: 'There is no danger of me doing that!' That may be the case, but there are others who enjoy their work and so can end up worshipping it. We can do that in different ways. It can become all-consuming and our only source of meaning and satisfaction. Who we are becomes utterly tied up with what we do. Our whole self-image and worth is derived from our work and we can end up living only to work and so being something of a workaholic.

For example, we may spend long days at the office or on the road with our mobile phone always on; we may be constantly checking emails - even finding internet cafés on holiday to go to. In doing so we are worshipping our work.

It might be the prestige or kudos; it might be the peer pressure or company work ethic; it might be the money or proving yourself a success, but nevertheless we are worshipping our work.

That is something the book of Ecclesiastes speaks about:

> *What do people get for all the toil and anxious striving with which they labour under the sun? All their days their work is grief and pain; even at night their minds do not rest. This too is meaningless.*
>
> *People can do nothing better than to eat and drink and find satisfaction in their toil. This too, I see, is from the hand of God, for without him, who can eat or find enjoyment?*
> (Ecc. 2:22-25)

We will not find full meaning and fulfilment in our work. Ecclesiastes is very clear on this: the person who lives only for their work has got it profoundly wrong. The need to appreciate work as a good and a worthwhile part of creation gives no excuse for living only to work. As the writer of Ecclesiastes comments, for those that do this, 'All their days their work is grief and pain; even at night their minds do not rest' (verse 23).

If that is our approach to work the writer is warning us that we have taken a good part of God's creation and lifted it way above the position it was supposed to have.

Notice in these verses though that the writer also says it is good to find what satisfaction you can in your work. He doesn't end up pouring scorn on work itself, only on those who live for their work. There is the right biblical view on work in a rebellious world. We look to get on with it and enjoy it when we can, but keep it in its rightful place.

So appreciate work as a good gift from God, and get on with it, but don't worship it, worship the God who made it.

Don't have a hierarchy of work

In Christian circles there is often an implicit hierarchy of work. It goes something like this. Christian work is the most valuable, worthwhile form of work, especially if you are a missionary or a minister. Then there are jobs with less value but which are still worthwhile: these may be healthcare jobs or aid work, and education is usually close behind. This is followed by everything else - those jobs we think of as purely secular, with no real value to them. Bottom of the pile is probably something finance-related (or being a traffic warden). Does this sound familiar?

But when we see God creating work in all its diversity there is no foundation for such a hierarchy. There are some things a Christian won't do as work - because it may be illegal or involve ethical issues. And we don't deny that there are differences in what different jobs achieve, but God created them all and they can be done to the glory of God. We see this when we read of the apostle Paul telling slaves to regard themselves as working for God whilst they are doing their menial tasks. And if that was true for them then, it is also true for all of us.

We must never think that the Christian worker glorifies God in their job and the person sweeping the street doesn't. We mustn't think of one job as 'spiritual' and another as 'unspiritual'. Similarly, we mustn't assess people on their job alone. We must not ask people what they do, and then slot them into our own hierarchy of worthiness.

Have balanced expectations of work

Christians who understand the biblical perspective on work should be the people who are simultaneously both the most positive and the most realistic about work. We saw this in chapter 2. We know how good it was made to be, we know how it's intrinsic to being human and is part of God's design, and so we're positive about it. We look to enjoy it where we can, and we do expect to find some satisfaction and delight in it.

But at the same time, we know how distorted it is and that it will never deliver the full satisfaction it was supposed to. Holding these two views in balance is important. It is this biblical view of work that provides us with realistic expectations and makes complete sense of our experience of work.

Being realistic is important. Some people have argued that because work is created by God, and because we are his people whom he loves and cares for, we should be able to find a great job that really suits us, and that is fulfilling and satisfying. Of course we can hope for that because we know God created work like that; but that line of thinking doesn't appreciate how devastating the effects of the Fall are, and so it's not realistic.

Our personalities come into play here as well. We have all been created differently. Some of us are perfectionists and some of us are clearly not! Perfectionism is a good trait in that it delights in work and wants to do it very well. But it can mean that you become unrealistic about the distortion of work in a fallen world. We need to recognize the effects of sin on work, and the fact that the 'ideal' we aim and long for may not be achieved; in this fallen world we will have to settle for less than perfection.

But for everyone, perfectionists or not, we should hold our view of work in balance. This means that we rejoice when work is good, and that we're not surprised when work is bad. The good times don't mean we worship it, and the bad times don't mean we despise it.

Have Jesus as Lord of your work

What does it mean to have Jesus as Lord? When we become Christians we repent and turn from our sins, placing ourselves under Jesus' Lordship and accepting his offer of forgiveness and reconciliation. So the Bible speaks of Christians as those who now belong to Jesus and who live for him.

Jesus being Lord applies to our work as much as to anything else. We will think through the practicalities of that in the next chapter. But for now ask yourself the following questions: Is Jesus Lord of my work? Is he Lord of my ambitions, my hopes? Am I prepared to hand everything over to him?

There is here, as with all of the Christian life, a very basic attitude of submission. So basic we often overlook it. We easily talk and sing about Jesus being Lord but we don't join the dots to connect that idea to working life. As a popular worship song challenges, do we surrender 'All' - whether that is our job, studies, domestic work, family life - into Jesus' hands?

> I heard the story of a man who decided that his work was taking over life; he was too busy with too many demands being made on him. He was aware his family was suffering and he was withdrawing from church responsibilities. He went to his boss and asked for a demotion; he wanted to go down the corporate ladder with the accompanying reduction in salary so that he was under less pressure.
>
> The thing that struck me most about that story was that someone was prepared to be so counterculural. Everyone else must have thought he was mad. But he was prepared to have Jesus as Lord in every area of his life, including his career.

Is Jesus Lord of your work? That might not mean asking for a demotion, but the change in attitude is huge. It means being prepared to go about your work as Jesus wants you to. It means being prepared to be as successful as Jesus would want you to be, rather than what you or others might want. It means getting on with the mundane nature of work and the responsibilities that you would prefer to skip. It might mean saying 'No' to certain business decisions because you know Jesus wouldn't approve of them. Or it might mean taking your studies seriously because you know Jesus wants you to. It will mean different things to each of us, but the question remains: is Jesus Lord of your work?

Let your work remind you of heaven

There will be times when work is frustrating, when it is an uphill battle with little satisfaction. In these situations what should we do? We should be reminded that this is a distorted world, and remind ourselves that this is not how it was meant to be. And so we can look forward to the day it will be redeemed.

When your work is getting you down, lift your eyes to the day when it will be a delight, the day when you will enjoy the work of your hands and you will not toil in vain. And in doing so, let your work remind you of heaven.

4

Working on Tuesday afternoon

What difference does being a Christian make to your working day? In the last chapter we looked at what we thought about our work. That is crucial because our understanding and thinking about work will shape how we go about it. But now we need to get practical and think about what we actually do differently.

The Apostle Paul talks about a regular working life in the letter to the Colossians. He is speaking about slaves and slave owners and how they should work. This is what he says:

> *Slaves, obey your earthly masters in everything; and do it, not only when their eye is on you and to curry their favour, but with sincerity of heart and reverence for the Lord. Whatever you do, work at it with all your heart, as working for the Lord, not for human masters, since you know that you will receive an inheritance from the Lord as a reward. It is the Lord Christ you are serving. Those who do wrong will be repaid for their wrongs, and there is no favoritism. Masters, provide your slaves with what is right and fair, because you know that you also have a Master in heaven.*
> Col. 3:22-4:1

When we hear the word 'slave' we tend to think of the barbaric slave trade of around the eighteenth century. What was happening in Paul's day was rather different -people had become bankrupt and so sold themselves or their families into slavery - they hadn't usually been kidnapped. However, they were still told what to do and could easily be mistreated.

But this arrangement of slaves and slave owners is the closest we have to our employee/employer relationship today, and Paul's words here really help us in knowing how to go about the practicalities of the working week. Let's look at this in more detail.

We are working for Jesus

Do you see that remarkable statement in verse 24? Paul says '…it is the Lord Christ you are serving.' Paul said that talking to slaves; those who usually had menial roles as domestic servants or labourers. And Paul says that they should think of themselves as being employed by Jesus. They should think of their daily work as service for Jesus. If Paul could say that to them, then we can apply this to any of us, no matter what our working life involves. As we discussed in the last chapter, we must remember that Jesus is our ultimate boss. For 'it is the Lord Christ I am serving.'

Maybe you're in a company with a chain of command all the way up to the Managing Director. You should think of Jesus as the real MD of your company. Maybe you're in the public sector with the council over your organization. Think of Jesus as Head of that council. Or it could be that you run your own business and you're in charge. Think of your business as being owned by Jesus, and that he's employing you to run it on his behalf. Perhaps you're in education. Think of Jesus as being your head-teacher or the Chancellor of your university.

Whether you are bringing up children, retired, doing voluntary work or whatever, think of Jesus as handing over those responsibilities to you.

You see we either think to ourselves, 'I work for Ford, or the council'; or we think 'I don't work for anyone, I'm my own boss.' Actually both are wrong. Whatever our situation, we should think of ourselves as serving Jesus Christ. He has given us the time we have and the duties we have and we are responsible to him for all that we do.

Think of Jesus as the one who's given out the original job description. He's put it in your hand, and said, 'That's what I want you to get on with.' In practice it might be worth writing out Colossians 3:24 - 'It is the Lord Christ you are serving' - and putting it somewhere that will remind you of this. As you think and pray about your work - whatever it is you do - you can bring that verse to mind. Let's get this clear: we are working for Jesus.

Put your heart into it

Paul writes: 'Whatever you do, work at it with all your heart, as working for the Lord, not for human masters, since you know that you will receive an inheritance from the Lord as a reward' (Col. 3:23-24).

There's a similar verse in Ephesians 6:7: 'Serve wholeheartedly as if you were serving the Lord, not people.' In other words, whatever you do, give yourself to it, put yourself into it. Don't just do the bare minimum to get by, and certainly don't be negligent or lazy. Don't be half-hearted, reluctant, but work wholeheartedly.

The slaves Paul was writing to in Colassae were forced to work hard. You might feel that pressure yourself - your boss may well be like a slave driver. Or you might experience financial pressures, or the threat of redundancy, or the lure of the bonus. Paul is telling us to put our heart into it not because we are forced to or have to, but because we are working for Jesus.

In other words, there is to be an inner motivation that's got nothing to do with outside constraints or pressures or temptations: that motivation and desire comes from the fact that we are serving the Lord Jesus. He is our ultimate employer and we want to please him. As Paul reminds us, we know that the final pay packet comes from him: 'you know that you will receive an inheritance from the Lord as a reward' (Col. 3:24). Whether we are rewarded well for our work now doesn't matter - we work wholeheartedly for Jesus; it is his reward that counts.

How can we apply this principle to our own situation? For those in paid employment it will mean working productively, not skimping and not skiving off. Or our work might be a mixture of childcare, shopping and domestic work. It is very easy to view these things as necessities that need to be done before we can do something more enjoyable. But this is not the case. We are to put our hearts into our work. Thinking of our work as the job that God has given us will change the way we view it.

It could be that you are retired or unemployed for some reason. What does the passage mean to you? The first application is to make sure you are working in some form or other, and that you are being productive, creative, and useful. For example, if you are retired you may still be able to get involved with a lunch club your church runs, or you may be able to visit the housebound and those who cannot make church on a Sunday. In fact there are numerous helpful and productive things that you can do in the life of the church and the community.

If you are unemployed you too will also have more time than those in employment will have. Of course there may be constraints on us because of illness or other factors - but in whatever time we have, with whatever energy we have, we should work at something. The world worships free time, but we know the Christian thinks differently.

Watch out for 'eye-service'

But Paul says, 'Slaves, obey your earthly masters in everything; and do it, not only when their eye is on you and to curry their favour, but with sincerity of heart and reverence for the Lord' (Col. 3:22).

Paul actually makes up a new word here. The phrase that is translated above 'when their eye is on you' is more literally 'eye-service'. You know what lip-service is - where you say one thing but mean another. Paul is talking about the visual equivalent to lip-service. In other words, 'Don't let your actions give the impression of working well when actually you're not.' Don't deceive your employer by pretending to work hard only when someone's watching.

I saw a cartoon on work where a manager was talking to an employee. He asked 'Why aren't you working?' The honest reply was, 'Because I didn't see you coming.' And the fact is that the quality of our work is so easily determined by who is watching. That is as true of any work - whether it is a project in the office, looking after our children, caring for a patient in hospital or doing a job in the church. Companies often have open-plan offices precisely because of this - it means a better work rate because people can see what you are doing. But the Christian shouldn't require such motivations.

Why? Because we know that we are working for Jesus. And in the Colossians passage Paul points out the positive difference that this should make. Verse 22 says we should work 'with sincerity of heart and reverence for the Lord.' Jesus knows how well we work, even if those around us don't. Our reverence for him in work means we work sincerely.

> Almost a couple of centuries ago Charles Spurgeon asked a maid what evidence there was that she had become a Christian. She replied, 'I now sweep under the mats.' The same principle applies today. Sincere work will mean doing things well even when people don't notice - because you know Jesus notices. It will mean a consistency and standard that is independent of a bonus or discipline.

There is one danger to guard against here. Don't take 'work sincerely' as meaning, 'have impossibly high standards you'll never achieve.' Watch out for the excessive hours at the office, or the constant cleaning in the home, where you are trying to achieve the impossible. It can be easy to justify such activity because you say, 'It's working for Jesus and so it has to be as good as it can be.' Working for Jesus sincerely simply means that there's no pretence about it; but it should not become obsessive.

There is another reason why we should work sincerely. As Paul tells his friend Titus, our attitude towards work can be a good witness for Jesus.

> *Teach slaves to be subject to their masters in everything, to try to please them, not to talk back to them, and not to steal from them, but to show that they can be fully trusted, so that in every way they will make the teaching about God our Saviour attractive.*
> Tit. 2:9-10

I remember someone at church asking me to pray for him one week because work was going to be hard. I asked him why, and he replied, 'Because the boss is away.' Everyone else would be taking it really easy that week and would be mocking him if he kept on working hard. If people know that we are Christians then we should also act as Christians. Don't underestimate the power of your witness.

Respect your employer

Not everyone has an actual employer, but most people in paid employment do. There are a number of Bible verses which talk about the obligation slaves have to respect their masters. For example, consider the two passages below:

All who are under the yoke of slavery should consider their masters worthy of full respect...
1 Tim. 6:1

Slaves, in reverent fear of God submit yourselves to your masters, not only to those who are good and considerate, but also to those who are harsh.
1 Pet. 2:18

We are to show respect to our 'masters'. A lot of slave owners weren't particularly worthy of respect; notice that Peter tells slaves to respect their masters no matter what they are like. It is not because they deserve it; rather it is because they hold an office of authority over you.

Paul and Peter also apply this principle when writing on other issues. For example, we are to respect and obey our rulers and our governments, not because they are worthy of respect, but because they have an office of authority. Elsewhere, children are told to honour and obey their parents - not because they are always good parents - but because they have an authority over you.

So how can we apply this principle of respecting those who have authority over us to our work situations today? Whilst the master-slave relationship is different to the employer-employee one, there are enough similarities for this to be instructive to us. We are to respect those who employ us or have authority over us. And we are to do so irrespective of whether the person above us is a good or a bad boss.

You may work somewhere where the coffee room sniping is difficult to avoid. There is mocking of the management or snide comments about the annoying boss. It's usually quite tempting to join in; and you can soon be considered on the wrong side if you don't - but too easily that involves not respecting those over us.

Of course, we are not blind to the faults of those above us, but we are still to respect them. We are to accept the tasks they give us willingly and work hard at them, even if those above us are not a good employer. Why? Because we are working for Jesus, and it is out of reverence for him. It is as if we look through our employer and see the Lord Jesus as the ultimate boss. And so we should be one of the best workers that our employer has.

There is of course a limit to our respect and obedience. The Christian doesn't bow to their boss when it would mean disobeying Christ. That clearly means there is some work Christians won't do and there is some business practices Christians won't accept. I know people who have been asked to lie for the sake of a business deal or misrepresent the accounts to save on taxes. As Christians they said 'No' to their boss. They said it respectfully but they said it nonetheless. In one case it even meant leaving a job. We should respect our employer, but we obey Jesus above employer.

Respect your employees

If you are an employer, or simply if there are people you manage in some way, Paul has some words for you as well. Many of us have people above and below us and so both these sections directly apply.

> *Masters, provide your slaves with what is right and fair, because you know that you also have a Master in heaven.*
> Col. 4:1

> *Masters, treat your slaves in the same way [that is with respect]. Do not threaten them, since you know that he who is both their Master and yours is in heaven, and there is no favouritism with him.*
> Eph. 6:9

These slave masters could actually do what they liked: they could treat people unfairly, be harsh and unkind. But Paul says working for Jesus changes all that. They must not think their position in authority means they can bear down on others or treat them how they want. Why? Because both slave and master are under a higher authority.

So he says don't threaten them, don't treat them unjustly; rather, give them what is right and fair. In other words don't abuse your authority. Today, even with employee rights, if you are someone's boss you have a lot of authority over them. You can affect their working life a great deal. Paul is saying don't abuse that position.

My mind casts back to the doctor I worked with who was respectful and kind to the nurses and the secretaries. He didn't snap at people or order them around; he thanked them for their contribution and appreciated their efforts. And so in a culture where such an attitude wasn't standard, he was known for his respect of those who he worked with.

> And what about us? Perhaps you have just got that promotion you were longing for, and now have a small team to manage. Don't be tempted to abuse your position and to assert your title. Or maybe you are second in command at a large flourishing business. Some believe that one day you will run it. Do people know that you are a Christian? Does this make any difference to the way that you work?

In fact the Christian boss should be the one who is known to be good to work for. The Christian boss is the one whose employees should say 'They get me working hard, but they respect me and they're always fair and considerate.' And you do so because you know your Father in heaven is looking down on you.

Live the normal Christian life - godliness

Whilst the passage from Colossians has been specifically about how we should work and our attitude towards it, there are other more general commands that we must transfer to the work place. Take, for example, earlier comments in Colossians 3 about putting to death anything that belongs to our old nature such as evil desires or greed and ridding ourselves of anger, slander and lies. Instead, Paul says, we are to 'put on' qualities such as love, compassion, patience and kindness (see Colossians 3:4-14).

Stop to think through the difference that those qualities could make to life in the work place. They don't so much affect how we do our work as to how we treat those we work with. These are all relational qualities that run against the average office dynamics.

'Putting on' these qualities means not joining in character assassination and gossip when backs are turned. It means not losing your temper with people when the deadline is looming or the proposal is rejected. It means being patient when a colleague is inconsiderate or annoying. Or it could mean not covering over mistakes or telling lies for the sake of our reputation. We are also to be understanding of others when they mess up. There are many ways in which we can apply these principles to our own situations. The key is to display a character of godliness.

Now of course we do not display these qualities by own merits - we are all sinful by nature, but if we are Christians then we have become new creations and we have the Holy Spirit living within us (2 Cor. 5:17). The Spirit is the one who now empowers us and leads us to live this godly life.

So in Galatians 5 Paul says that the Christian should live by the Spirit and so produce his fruit - the qualities of love and kindness and gentleness we've been thinking about. Living by the Spirit is set in contrast to living by the sinful nature which will produce things like hatred, discord, selfish ambition and fits of rage.

The work place is the battleground where this is put into practice just as much as anywhere in life. How much are we showing the fruit of the Spirit at work? Are we asking for the empowering and leading of the Spirit as we walk into the office? If not, can we expect to be any different?

My wife and I recently watched The Apprentice - the programme where the successful business man Alan Sugar whittles down a group of prospective applicants to one person who will finally work for him. It is engaging TV, seeing how the applicants cope with the tasks they are set each week, and how they try to promote or defend themselves. However, it is an environment that usually results in the very opposite of Christian godliness. People think well only of themselves and put others down; they often lie or mislead; greed and ambition underlies it all.

And while that is a hot-house version, the same can be true within many a business setting. Here the Christian has to live out the normal Christian life - a life of godliness. And that includes when the going gets tough. It is easy when everything is going well for us. But our reactions to when things go wrong are often an indication of our true character. Let's ask the Holy Spirit to convict and challenge us about our attitudes and reactions to things so that we may continually be a good witness at work.

Go home

As we have seen, working for Jesus does mean we work well, put our heart into it and are sincere; but the fact that we're working for him, not ourselves or our employers, means we go home.

Knowing we are working for Jesus also means we keep work in the proper place. It means we view it correctly, and don't let it dominate. It's very easy to work hard because we enjoy it or we get credibility out of it, or our self-image may be bound up with it. That's back to worshipping the work and not the one who made it.

In remembering we are working for Jesus we focus on the bigger picture. Back in Genesis God worked and then rested, setting the model for us to follow. We should not feel guilty during our time off. And we should not neglect those other parts of our lives - our friends, family, church life and other commitments. We need to live a balanced life.

So we are not to take 'put your heart into it' as meaning, 'do nothing but work', because Jesus calls you to more than that. Don't take 'respect your employer' as meaning 'work all the hours they'd like you to'; Jesus has given you other responsibilities as well, and he's your ultimate boss.

We can go home after a day's work with a clear conscience, knowing that we have worked hard for our Lord and Saviour. We can face another day of 'hard toil and labour' because we know that we were created to rule and work. We can pray for the right attitude as we face struggles and hardships, knowing that the Holy Spirit is with us and will help us and equip us. And we can look forward to that glorious day when the Lord Jesus will return again bringing about a new creation, where we will be at 'home' with him.

So let us continue to spur each other on.

Live all of life - including your work - under Jesus as your Lord.

Further reading

90,000 Hours: Managing the World of Work, Rodney Green
(Milton Keynes: Scripture Union, 2002)

Glory Days: Living the Whole of Your Life for Jesus, Julian Hardyman
(IVP: Nottingham, 2006)

God's Payroll: Whose Work is it Anyway? Neil Hood
(Milton Keynes: Authentic Media, 2003)

Thank God it's Monday, Mark Greene
(Milton Keynes: Scripture Union, 2001)

The Busy Christian's Guide to Busyness, Tim Chester
(IVP: Nottingham, 2006)

Work and Leisure in Christian Perspective, Leland Ryken
(IVP: Nottingham, 1990)

10 OF THOSE.COM
THE best way to buy CHRISTIAN books in bulk

For more copies of this booklet go to **www.10ofthose.com**

We carry a wide selection of books – theology, biography, Christian lifestyle, Bibles and commentaries all at guaranteed low prices.

We service many church bookstalls around the UK and can help your church to set up a bookstall.

Single and bulk purchases welcome. For more information contact:
quote@10ofthose.com

10ofthose.com is a not-for-profit limited company.

www.10ofthose.com